WHAT'S HIDDEN IN THE SKY

ANIMAL CONSTELLATIONS AROUND THE WORLD

Aina Bestard

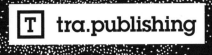

On a cloudless night, if you're out in nature, far from the city, and you look at the sky, you will see that it's full of stars.

Many years ago, the ancient Greeks enjoyed contemplating and studying the stars as they shone in the night sky.
They named each star and grouped them together in the shapes of animals, objects, and mythological characters.
These groups of stars are called constellations.

THE STARS YOU SEE EACH NIGHT ARE NOT THE SAME, NOR ARE THEY IN THE SAME PLACE.

Since the universe is in constant movement and the Earth turns on its axis, what we see depends on where we are and the time of year.

On the same summer night, a child in Japan will see different stars than a child in New Zealand.

HOW THIS BOOK WORKS:

This book takes you inside children's homes around the world.
When you open the window in each room, you'll see the stars.

If you hold the window on each page up to a light source,
an animal constellation will appear. Guess which animal
by answering the accompanying riddle.

1.

KYOTO
Japan

MARCH 4

As the cat takes a nap, the night draws near.
And if you look closely, in the sky this appears.
It lives in the forest and sleeps in the winter.
It's a large furry mammal, heavy and gentle.

2.

OUARZAZATE
Morocco

JULY 18

At the desert's door, summer gets underway;
a huge bird you'll see if you keep sleep at bay.
Open the window to the unending heat.
You will see its huge wings and big, curving beak.

King of the jungle during the day;
by night, he's a guide who'll
show you the way.
Don't give up; search the
stars as they shine.
High in the heavens, you'll
find this feline.

In the summer night skies you will be enthralled
by the bird who is the most regal of all.
When it spreads its tail, a most glorious fan,
its colors greet you like a waving hand.

In olden times, this long-necked mammal
was thought to be a mix of leopard and camel.
High in the starry skies of the night,
this savannah dweller blazes bright.

Creatures in river and stream,
in the night sky they gleam.
Agile swimmers in many hues.
If you can guess—good for you!

7

Camelopardalis
The giraffe

Brightest star:
Beta Camelopardalis

Camelopardalis is a large constellation in the Northern Hemisphere. It's difficult to see because none of its stars are particularly bright.

Beta Camelo-pardalis

1

KYOTO / Japan

Ursa Major
The bear

Brightest star: **Alioth**

Containing the cluster of stars known as the **Big Dipper**, well known for its ladle-like shape, this is the most famous constellation in the Northern Hemisphere, where it is visible all year long.

Alioth

3

GUADALAJARA / Mexico

Leo
The lion

Brightest star: **Régulo**

This is one of the constellations in the Zodiac, and contains many bright stars.

The Leo constellation takes the form of a lion's head and body, separated by a mane.

It can easily be seen in the Northern Hemisphere during the spring months.

Régulo

6

LAMU / Kenya

Pavo
The peacock

Brightest star: **Alfa Pavonis**

The Pavo constellation may be seen from countries in the Southern Hemisphere, primarily during the summer months.

Peacock

5

ZALESIE / Poland

Vulpecula
The fox

Brightest star: **Anser**

Vulpecula is a constellation visible in the Northern Hemisphere. It's located in the Summer Triangle and is part of the Milky Way.

Anser